True colors

jodi hills

TRISTAN Publishing

Minneapolis

To Brody, Micah, Quinn and Charly,

Your great-great-grandmother made beautiful quilts that I still use today. Your great-grandmother made an orange book bag for me when I was six that made me fall in love with color and words. Neither of them taught me how to sew, so this book is my gift to you. Love the world in your own colorful ways.

Love, Jodi

Library of Congress Cataloging-in-Publication Data

Hills, Jodi
True colors / Written by Jodi Hills.
pages cm
ISBN 978-1-939881-00-7 (alk. paper)
I. Title.
PS3608.I454T78 2013
811'.6--dc23
2013010194

TRISTAN Publishing, Inc.
2355 Louisiana Avenue North
Golden Valley, MN 55427

ISBN 978-1-939881-00-7
First Printing
Printed in China

It never occurred to me to have a favorite color.

They are all so **beautiful!**

I used to wake up at 6 a.m. on Saturday mornings
to watch cartoons. It was all about the colors—

so vibrant,
so filling,
so stimulating!

I wanted to get closer and closer.
I could feel the colors dance inside my heart and mind.
I knew that I was witnessing something magical.

I heard, "Don't get too close, back up from the screen." So I did—right into a box of crayons! There was that magic again. First the box of 18, then 36, then 64—the possibilities multiplied. I colored and mixed and tore back the paper and colored some more.

What a beautiful gift, these colors! I heard, "Stay inside the lines." That would be impossible, I thought.

You can't contain magic.

The certainty of youth is bright, but living can dim almost anyone. I was determined not to become one of them.

I was determined to **live in color.**

I was determined to get too close, to see too much, to peel back the boundaries and run outside the lines and live— to live in all the beautiful colors.

And that's when I met you. There was that magic again!

You, all 6 a.m. wide awake,

dancing off the screen, off the page.

I knew it. This was living color.

You are living color!

Your colors—the purple passions and reds on fire! The greens of growth and the warmth of blues. The indecision of grays and the strength of browns. Wishing whites and playful pinks, golden hopes and silver dreams.

Rainbows smile with slight envy, and so do I, as you move with such comfort and ease on your untraveled path.

What a thrill it is to see you.

I see you and I see joy—not to confuse that with happiness. Yes, you convey happiness, but it's more than that.

I've seen you laugh, and I've seen you cry. I've seen you on shoulders and on knees. And through it all, your colors have never dimmed. You are lit from within, and it shines through your smile!

So unique and so bold, your light shines so brightly—
but not with disregard for others. It never feels like you are
saying, "Hey, look at me," but more, "Hey, look at everybody!"
"Look at all these beautiful people!"

You've never been one to exclude. You have been one to invite!
You are an invitation to see all, to see everyone's true colors.

And I accept!

I know there's a responsibility in that. Once you've seen someone, seen their true colors, you're involved. You can no longer just blend—you must be! Be a part of all the colors—

however messy, however magical—

because that's where the beauty lives.

You are such a gift to the fearful drabness of this world.

And wow! That takes courage!

It takes so much courage to be colorful. Your colors say that we are supposed to be brave, that we are supposed to be different, that we are supposed to collect the colors from cartoons and crayons and create our own beauty.

Your colors shout that it's not just okay to be different. It's more than okay—**it's beautiful.** I wonder if you know what a gift that is.

I wonder if you know, just by being you, you give that gift to me, and to so many. You do! Know it! You bring color to this world.

Color does not separate, it connects. We are all offered the brilliant yellows of 6 a.m., the comforting blues of midnight, and the ever-changing greens that grow in-between.

All of our possibilities lie in these colors. They allow us to take chances, to be open, to be creative, and to be **accepting of all.**

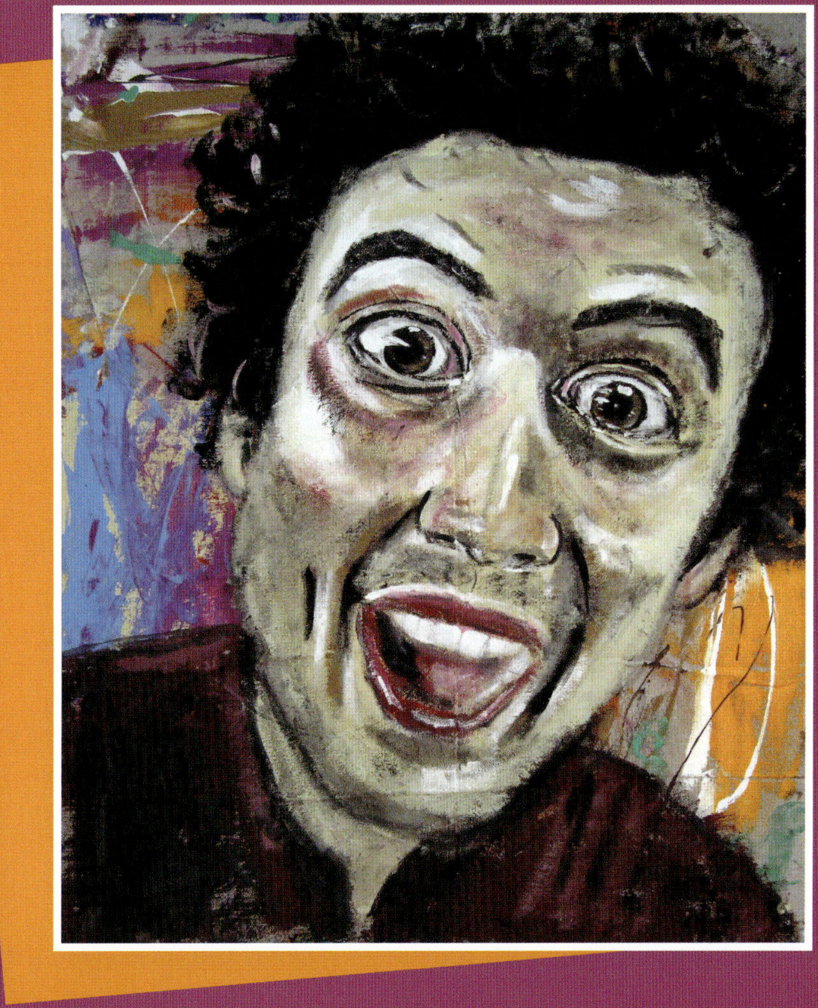

Because of you, I will not wear my own true colors timidly. I will paint them on the sides of buildings, the corners of wrapped canvas, the spines of books, and the hearts of children. Because of you, I see how important it is to **never fade**. We must invent and **illuminate**. We must mix and strengthen. We must break boundaries and build bridges. We must entertain and console. You do!

Every day, you show by example that it's not only so valuable to live this way, but that it can be so joyful, too. How dull would it be to live in a world where everyone was the same?

I want to live brilliantly, vibrantly—not like you, but along with you!

And there it is. I understand now. I really see.

It’s not the color of your face, but all that you have faced.

You are the sum of all colors. We are the sum of all colors. We are the boxes of 18, 36, and 64, and we're all in this together. Oh, the beauty! The golden flecks of inquisitive eyes, the pastel tears of overwhelming joy, the pink-surrounded toothy grins, the pulsing blues of racing veins, and the **vibrant reds of the beats that carry us all.**

You're smiling at me now—the way I go on!

I guess in my own colorful way, I just wanted to say thank you. Thanks for being brave and different. Thanks for breathing the certainty of youth. Thanks for showing me that nothing adds more color than joy and nothing adds more joy than color.

Thanks for not following. Thanks for dancing off the screen and off the page, for going outside the lines! Thanks for being alive—

and I mean ALIVE!

Thanks for giving me the opportunity to see your true colors, the wisdom to see others' and **the courage to see my own.**

Truly, I give thanks for this and you,

every colorful day!